⭐ WEAPONS OF WAR
SMALL ARMS
1950 TO TODAY

A⁺
Smart Apple Media

Published by arrangement with Amber Books

Contributing authors: Chris Chant, Steve Crawford, Martin J. Dougherty,
Ian Hogg, Robert Jackson, Chris McNab, Michael Sharpe, Philip Trewhitt

Special thanks to series consultant Dr. Steve Potts

Photo credits: Art-Tech/Aerospace, Cody Images, Corbis, U.S. Department of Defense

Illustrations: © Art-Tech/Aerospace

Library of Congress Cataloging-in-Publication Data

McNab, Chris, 1970-
Small arms : 1950 to today / Chris McNab.
pages cm. — (Weapons of war)
Includes Index.
ISBN 978-1-62588-046-8
1. Firearms — History — 20th century. 2. Firearms — History — 20th century. I. Title.
UD380.M45 2015
623.4'4 — dc23
                                2013032033

Printed in the United States at Corporate Graphics,
North Mankato, Minnesota
PO1649
2-2014

9 8 7 6 5 4 3 2 1

CONTENTS

Introduction

Modern Guns

Modern small arms are more potent than ever, putting massive firepower at the disposal of individual soldiers.

The term "small arms" was coined long ago to describe firearms that could be carried by a single person, i.e., gunpowder weapons lighter than artillery. Over the years, distinct types of small arms began to appear, each optimized to a particular role. The line between artillery and small arms was blurred when firearms heavy enough to be considered as support weapons began to appear. Light enough to move with infantry units, but more potent than standard personal weapons, battlefield support weapons greatly increased the firepower of an infantry force.

The invention of personal automatic weapons was another profound leap forward. Where previously, group action was necessary to provide intense firepower, now

KALASHNIKOV AK: see pages 34-35

M16: see page 36

L1A1 SLR: see page 33

WEAPONS OF WAR

The increased frequency of urban combat has hugely influenced the development of modern small arms.

a single individual could target multiple opponents or deliver suppressing fire into an area. The increasing frequency of urban combat during World War II was another influence on the development of small arms and infantry support weapons. While previously most engagements were at relatively long ranges of several hundred yards, which required accurately aimed rifle fire, urban battles were characterized by vicious short-range firefights. During the Battle of Stalingrad in WWII, for example,

German troops armed with bolt-action rifles found themselves outgunned in such engagements by the Soviet Union's Red Army soldiers who were armed with submachine guns. Swapping rifles for submachine guns would have been an effective counter for urban combat, but in longer-range engagements, the rifle was still the weapon of choice. The answer was an intermediate weapon: smaller, lighter, and faster firing than the traditional battle rifle, but still retaining good accuracy out

H&K G3: see page 37

FAMAS: see page 38

to a respectable range, with reasonable penetrating power. Thus was born the assault rifle and with it came a change in emphasis from groups of riflemen trained to a high standard of marksmanship towards smaller units capable of delivering intense firepower within their local vicinity.

COMBAT EFFECTIVENESS

A group of militia or gunmen will normally fight as individuals with whatever weapons they can get, but formal military forces are organized in a way that optimizes the effectiveness of their weapons. Various approaches have been tried in order to obtain maximum combat effectiveness, and the success of one does not necessarily mean another is wrong.

Typically, an infantry squad consists mainly of riflemen armed with a basic personal weapon, usually an assault rifle. The squad will normally have a support weapon of some kind. This may be a general-purpose machine gun (GPMG) or a lighter squad support weapon. GPMGs tend to be chambered for battle rifle calibers; their ammunition is not compatible with the lighter cartridges used in assault weapons. However, GPMGs are powerful and offer good sustained firepower, with the ability to reach distances that lighter weapons cannot.

Squad (or light) support weapons are sometimes little more than a variation of the standard infantry rifle, which has the advantage that magazines can be shared, and any soldier can take over the support weapon. Mobility is better, too, since the weapon is lighter. However, a light support weapon does not have the hitting power or the sustained firepower of a GPMG.

BERETTA MODEL 92SB: see page 26

STERLING L2A1: see page 44

Other weapons are generally used for supporting purposes. Handguns are carried as sidearms, shotguns are primarily used for security (and sometimes counter-ambush) applications, and an infantry force may be supported by grenade launchers and/or personnel armed with extremely accurate and often high-powered precision rifles.

Other approaches have been used, and successfully. For example, Chinese forces in the Korean War made extensive use of massed submachine guns in the assault role, while the British Army long considered marksmanship with a semi-automatic rifle more effective than automatic suppressive fire.

ASSAULT RIFLE SUPREME

With the end of World War II, most major powers were starting to recognize that the best infantry weapon would be the assault rifle, situated as it was between the pistol-

WEAPONS OF WAR

BERETTA MODEL 12: see page 46

caliber, short-range submachine gun and the long-range rifle. In 1947, the most famous assault rifle of all time was produced by Mikhail Timofeyevich Kalashnikov — the AK-47. It fired a 7.62mm intermediate cartridge and impressed the world with its ability to deliver heavy individual firepower while enduring the worst battlefield conditions.

Although it would later catch up, the newly formed North Atlantic Treaty Organization (NATO) countries missed a bold chance to match the AK-47's useful cartridge with something similar by agreeing to standardize all NATO weapons to 7.62 x 51mm NATO. This round was too powerful for an assault rifle with automatic capabilities, but some of the US military was reluctant to give up the long-range round. Many fine weapons were produced for this caliber — the US M14, the superb FN FAL and Heckler & Koch's G3 — but they all struggled under fully automatic fire.

A better solution had begun to emerge from the US shortly after the Korean War. Research had begun into small-caliber high-velocity (1000mps/3200fps) ammunition, specifically the 5.56mm round. A rifle to fire this round was found in Eugene Stoner's AR-15, which would become the M16 rifle after it was adopted by the US Air Force in the early 1960s. The M16 used a highly efficient gas-operation and could fire easily on full automatic. Furthermore, the velocity of the small round was such that it retained the stopping and killing power of much larger rounds by force of its supersonic shock effect.

The 5.56mm round was resisted for many years (its cause not helped by early jamming problems with the M16), yet, after

UZI: see page 45

WEAPONS OF WAR

L7A1: see page 50

PKM 7.62MM: see page 52

the US Army adopted it for general use in the M16A1 during the Vietnam War, its acceptance was assured. In the late 1970s, the Soviet Union brought out a 5.45mm version of the AK-47, the AK-74; after trials in the 1980s, the 5.56 x 45mm round was adopted as the NATO standard.

Bullpup designs also gained currency. These were weapons that located much of the receiver behind the trigger unit and thus were able to maximize the length of the barrel for accuracy, while restraining the overall length of the weapon. Some of these designs have become standard-issue infantry weapons in some armies.

OTHER WEAPONS

While assault rifles have generally eclipsed submachine guns in their prominence following World War II, submachine gun technology and designs also continued to improve. Perhaps the greatest development is in the area of compaction. High-quality submachine guns such as the Heckler & Koch MP5 series retain more rifle-like proportions, but other submachine guns have become little bigger than pistols. By siting the magazine within the pistol grip and using a telescoping bolt (i.e. a bolt which actually encloses the end of the barrel), guns such as the Uzi, the Ingram M10, and the South African BXP are easily concealed, yet can spray out devastating firepower in close-combat situations.

At the other end of the scale, standard assault rifles have also been developed with longer, heavier barrels to become squad automatic weapons (SAWs). These are intended to give small infantry units greater sustained-fire capability and range with

M60: see page 48

WEAPONS OF WAR

MINIGUN: see page 53

Some standard assault rifles have been developed as squad automatic weapons to provide supporting fire for infantry units.

their standard caliber weapons and from standard magazines. The jury is still out as to whether they perform a more valuable function over the general purpose machine gun (GPMG) type that has been used as a heavier support weapon by most armies since World War II.

The astonishing scientific progress in terms of ballistics, materials, and manufacturing in the twentieth and twenty-first centuries means that even the humble pistol is a work of mastery. Modern handguns

such as the SIG-Sauer P226 have 15-round magazines or, like the Glock pistol range, a higher percentage of their build in plastic than in metal. Sniper rifles have gone even further. The contemporary sniper armed with, say, an FR-F1 or an L96A1, and looking through an advanced-optics telescopic sight can confidently expect a first-round kill at 874 yards (800 m), while, in the Gulf War, a sniper armed with a Barrett .50-caliber rifle took a confirmed kill at 1968 yards (1800 m). The US military

REMINGTON M870: see page 57

uses the XM2010 Enhanced Sniper Rifle which has a range of 1500 yards (1370 m).

THE FUTURE

The big question is, what next? In terms of weapons that use conventional ammunition and methods of operation, we have perhaps gone as far as we can. Recent experiments have been conducted using machine guns that fire bullets through electromagnetic acceleration rather than percussion, the result being an utterly silent, yet astonishingly dense and powerful rain of high-velocity fire. Other ideas are already off the drawing board. Heckler & Koch's G11 rifle fires caseless ammunition in which the bullet is embedded in a rectangle of propellant that disappears completely on firing. The removal of the need for ejection gives the rifle a very high rate of fire — its three-round burst sounds as a single explosion. Electro-magnetic propulsion weapons, however, might one day do away with propellants altogether. As history has shown, progress in weapons design is inevitable, and the next stage will soon be with us. In the final analysis, although the capabilities of a weapon are important, what really matters is the user. Good tactics and skilled marksmanship can overcome the limitations of a mediocre weapon system. It is when training, tactics, and fighting spirit are combined with an effective weapon that success on the battlefield is achieved.

BARRETT M82A1: see page 40

Smith & Wesson Model 29 .44 Magnum

The power of the .44 Magnum handgun gained particular notoriety in the hands of Clint Eastwood in the 1970s, through his role in the popular "Dirty Harry" movies (although Smith & Wesson actually launched the Model 29 back in 1955). The Model 29 came with a choice of three barrel lengths, ranging from the shortest — a 4.29 in (102 mm) version — to a striking 7.99 in (203 mm) version (which appeared in the films, and to which the specifications shown refer). Production of the Model 29 by Smith & Wesson has continued to this day in several different versions, now mostly designated as the 629 series. Most of the Model 29/629 series are distinguished by finish (the 629 first came out in stainless steel in 1979), barrel length or the positioning of the ejector rod, which is either shrouded or set into a recess underneath the barrel.

SPECIFICATIONS
COUNTRY OF ORIGIN: United States
CALIBER: .44 Magnum
LENGTH: 13.89 inches (353 mm)
WEIGHT: 3.19 pounds (1.45 kg)
BARREL: 203 mm, 6 grooves, rh; also 153 mm or 102 mm
FEED: 6 rounds
OPERATION: revolver
MUZZLE VELOCITY: 1476 fps (450 mps)
EFFECTIVE RANGE: 164 feet (50 m)
CYCLIC RATE OF FIRE: not applicable

Heckler & Koch P9

The Heckler & Koch P9 comes in two versions: the standard P9 which is a single-action pistol (operation of the internal hammer is achieved by a release and cocking lever on the left side of the frame) and the P9S, which is a double-action weapon. What both have in common, however, is that they use the Heckler & Koch roller-locked delayed blowback system used in the G3 assault rifle. Thus, as recoil drives the bolt system rearwards, two rollers lock into barrel extensions and hold the bolt until pressure is at a safe level. Both the P9 and PS9 are fine handguns, used by several police and military units around the world; .45 caliber (for the US market) and 7.65 mm Parabellum versions have also been issued. One item of note is that the bore has a polygonal configuration, with the rifling grooves set into the bore diameter.

SPECIFICATIONS

COUNTRY OF ORIGIN: Germany
CALIBER: .45 ACP or 9 mm Parabellum
LENGTH: 7.56 inches (192 mm)
WEIGHT: 1.94 pounds (0.88 kg)
BARREL: 102 mm, polygonal, rh
FEED: 9-round detachable box (9 mm); 7-rnd detach. box (.45 ACP)
OPERATION: roller-locked delayed blowback
MUZZLE VELOCITY: 1150 fps (350 mps)
EFFECTIVE RANGE: 131 feet (40 m)
CYCLIC RATE OF FIRE: not applicable

Walther P5

The Walther P5 was produced by the company in the 1970s to meet the demanding safety criteria of the West German police, who were looking for a new handgun. The gun's actual firing mechanism is essentially that of the excellent Walther P38, but with three specific safety features. First, only if the trigger is pulled, will the firing pin strike the cartridge, as usually the firing pin sits in a recess in the hammer; pulling the trigger realigns the firing pin with the impact portion of the hammer. Added to this is a safety notch for the hammer, and the gun will not fire unless the slide is in a fully closed position. In addition to its first-class safety precautions, the P5 is also a splendid weapon to fire, and its overall fine qualities have taken it into service outside Germany, in countries such as Portugal and Holland.

SPECIFICATIONS

COUNTRY OF ORIGIN: Germany
CALIBER: 9 mm Parabellum
LENGTH: 7.08 inches (180 mm)
WEIGHT: 1.75 pounds (0.79 kg)
BARREL: 90 mm, 6 grooves, rh
FEED: 8-round detachable box magazine
OPERATION: short recoil
MUZZLE VELOCITY: 1150 fps (350 mps)
EFFECTIVE RANGE: 131 feet (40 m)
CYCLIC RATE OF FIRE: not applicable

Glock 17

A remarkable weapon in terms of construction, materials, and marketing, the Glock 17 has become a dominant force in the military and commercial handgun industries since its introduction. First produced in 1983, it demonstrates a 40 percent use of plastic materials (although the barrel and slide naturally remain metal) and an inventory of only 33 parts for each gun. While the plastic makes it a light weapon, the Glock 17 also has an impressive magazine capacity of no less than 17 rounds and fires its ammunition using a trigger-controlled striker instead of a hammer. It uses a locked breech with tilting barrel mechanism and safety is provided by a trigger safety and firing-pin lock. Through good marketing, and following its adoption by the Austrian Army, the Glock 17 has gone on to extensive military and police use across the world.

SPECIFICATIONS
COUNTRY OF ORIGIN: Austria
CALIBER: 9 mm Parabellum
LENGTH: 7.40 inches (188 mm)
WEIGHT: 1.44 pounds (0.65 kg)
BARREL: 114 mm, 6 grooves, rh
FEED: 17-round detachable box magazine
OPERATION: short recoil
MUZZLE VELOCITY: 1148 fps (350 mps)
EFFECTIVE RANGE: 131 feet (40 m)
CYCLIC RATE OF FIRE: n/a

Beretta Model 92SB

The Beretta Model 92SB had the honor of winning the US Army's trials in the 1980s for a replacement side arm to the M1911, although some further modifications had to be made before it went into US service as the Model 92F. The 92SB is actually part of an extensive Model 92 series, all of superb quality and designed around a practical range of military and security needs. Origins of the 92 series began in an update of the Model 951 with a greater magazine capacity and a double action. Subsequent models improved on various elements and, by the time the 92SB reached the US trials, it had an ambidextrous safety and magazine catch and a half-cock facility. The 92F saw further modifications to satisfy US purchase demands, mainly limited to the gun's ergonomics, but also including the internal chroming of the barrel.

SPECIFICATIONS
COUNTRY OF ORIGIN: Italy
CALIBER: 9 mm Parabellum
LENGTH: 7.76 inches (197 mm)
WEIGHT: 2.16 pounds (0.98 kg)
BARREL: 109 mm, 6 grooves, rh
FEED: 13-round detachable box magazine
OPERATION: short recoil
MUZZLE VELOCITY: 385 mps (1263 fps)
EFFECTIVE RANGE: 131 feet (40 m)
CYCLIC RATE OF FIRE: not applicable

Star 30M

The he Star 30M is an exceptional pistol, which first entered production in 1990 and is still going strong today in various commercial and military hands. On first glance, the 30M actually looks like a standard Browning imitation gun, but further examination shows that the weapon's slide is actually running inside the gun's frame instead of outside. This configuration gives the gun great stability when it is being fired, and therefore increased accuracy. The resultant performance and the double-action trigger system enabled the 30M to take a contract for a Spanish Army service pistol and it is likely that this excellent design will open up many export markets for Astra in the future. In addition to the all-steel 30M, there is a light alloy version available on the market known as the 30PK, which has a lighter overall weight.

SPECIFICATIONS

COUNTRY OF ORIGIN: Spain
CALIBER: 9 mm Parabellum
LENGTH: 8.07 inches (205 mm)
WEIGHT: 2.51 pounds (1.14 kg)
BARREL: 119 mm, 6 grooves, rh
FEED: 15-round detachable box magazine
OPERATION: blowback
MUZZLE VELOCITY: 1250 fps (380 mps)
EFFECTIVE RANGE: 131 feet (40 m)
CYCLIC RATE OF FIRE: not applicable

Smith & Wesson 1006

During the 1980s, Smith & Wesson introduced a Third Generation series of pistols in various calibers ranging from 9 mm to .45 ACP and including, in the case of the 1006, a 10 mm Auto weapon. This was not the first 10 mm development in the history of handguns — the US company Dornaus & Dixon produced one, the Bren 10, in the early 1980s — but this ceased production when the company went into receivership in 1985. By this time, however, the FBI were interested in the potential of the 10 mm gun and so Smith & Wesson produced the 1006 starting in 1990. The caliber makes the gun very powerful indeed, but good-quality Novak sights and combat grips make it controllable in trained hands. The numbering system is part of Smith & Wesson's Third Generation notation, the first two digits indicating the caliber of the weapon.

SPECIFICATIONS

COUNTRY OF ORIGIN: United States
CALIBER: 10 mm Auto
LENGTH: 8.50 inches (216 mm)
WEIGHT: 2.37 pounds (1.07 kg)
BARREL: 127 mm, 6 grooves, rh
FEED: short recoil
OPERATION: 9-round detachable box magazine
MUZZLE VELOCITY: 1100 fps (335 mps)
EFFECTIVE RANGE: 98 feet (30 m)
CYCLIC RATE OF FIRE: not applicable

M40A1

The M40 was a specific selection of the US Marine Corps in 1966 and is essentially a standard Remington Model 700 adapted for military use. The M40 was a superb weapon by all accounts and authorities, and met the high standards placed on it by the exhaustively trained Marine snipers. It featured a Mauser-type bolt action and a heavy barrel, with a five-round magazine. The M40A1 is an improved version of this gun. The heavy barrel has given way to a stainless steel barrel and the furniture is now made out of the lighter fiberglass, rather than wood, which improves its handling. In addition, whereas the M40 used a Redfield zoom telescopic sight that could reach x 9 magnification, the latest sight climbs to x 10 magnification. This sight obviates the need for the iron sight fitting that can be seen on some of the earliest M40 models.

SPECIFICATIONS

COUNTRY OF ORIGIN: United States
CALIBER: 7.62 x 51 mm NATO
LENGTH: 43.98 inches (1117 mm)
WEIGHT: 14.48 pounds (6.57 kg)
BARREL: 610 mm, 4 grooves, rh
FEED: 5-round integral box magazine
OPERATION: bolt action
MUZZLE VELOCITY: 2550 fps (777 mps)
EFFECTIVE RANGE: 2624 feet (800 m) plus
CYCLIC RATE OF FIRE: not applicable

Steyr SSG 69

When the Steyr SSG 69 emerged as the Austrian Army's standard sniper rifle in 1969, it soon gathered a reputation as a well-crafted, robust, and especially accurate bolt-action weapon. Equipped with the x 6 Kahles ZF69 sight, it could not only achieve a guaranteed first-round kill at 2624 feet (800 m), but it could also then place the next 10 rounds in a grouping of less than 15.75 inches (400 mm) at the same range (the SSG 69 subsequently went on to be an internationally competitive target rifle). Being Austrian in origin, the SSG 69 had to be strong enough for use by mountain troops. The bolt action is of a rear-locking Mannlicher type using six locking lugs and it uses the pre–World War I Mannlicher rotary magazine (a standard 10-round box is also applicable), both unusual choices for a modern gun, but very strong in design. The SSG 69 is fully adjustable, including stock length.

SPECIFICATIONS
COUNTRY OF ORIGIN: Austria
CALIBER: 7.62 x 51 mm NATO
LENGTH: 44.88 inches (1140 mm)
WEIGHT: 8.59 pounds (3.9 kg)
BARREL: 650 mm, 4 grooves, rh
FEED: 5-round rotary or 10-round box magazine
OPERATION: bolt action
MUZZLE VELOCITY: 2820 fps (860 mps)
EFFECTIVE RANGE: 3280 feet (1000 m)
CYCLIC RATE OF FIRE: not applicable

Accuracy International L96A1

The L96A1 entered production in 1985 as the replacement for the Lee-Enfield L42A1 as the British Army and the UK Marine's standard sniper rifle. It continues in 7.62 mm NATO caliber, but, being descended from the Model PM — an Olympic-standard sports rifle — it has a new level of sophistication for a combat sniper weapon. The free-floating stainless steel barrel and Tasco sight give a 100 per cent hit rate at 1968 feet (600 m), while the stock is designed for ambidextrous use. The rifle is fitted with an alloy bipod and both rifle stripping and barrel change are simple tasks. Variants of the L96A1 include versions chambered for 7 mm Remington Magnum, the .300 Winchester Magnum and .338 Lapua Magnum (rounds that give extra range), a single-shot long-range version and a silenced version, which uses subsonic ammunition.

SPECIFICATIONS

COUNTRY OF ORIGIN: United Kingdom
CALIBER: 7.62 mm NATO and others
LENGTH: 45.78 inches (1163 mm)
WEIGHT: 13.68 pounds (6.2 kg)
BARREL: 654 mm, 4 grooves, rh
FEED: 10-round detachable box magazine
OPERATION: bolt action
MUZZLE VELOCITY: 2830 fps (840 mps)
EFFECTIVE RANGE: 3280 feet (1000 m)
CYCLIC RATE OF FIRE: n/a

Beretta Sniper

Despite being a rather conventional rifle, the Beretta Sniper still possesses a very good performance, due in the main to Beretta's superb standards of workmanship and engineering. What it does have, however, is an advanced free-floating barrel design, in which a counterweight in the forestock serves almost to cancel out barrel vibrations upon firing for even greater accuracy. Generally used in a sniper role with the standard-issue Zeiss Divari Z telescopic sights, it can also be fitted with precision iron sights, which are capable of telling use in trained hands. The Beretta Sniper has not achieved great sales outside of Italian security use and its production has now been discontinued.

SPECIFICATIONS

COUNTRY OF ORIGIN: Italy
CALIBER: 7.62 x 51 mm NATO
LENGTH: 45.87 inches (1165 mm)
WEIGHT: 12.23 pounds (5.55 kg)
BARREL: 586 mm, 4 grooves, rh
FEED: 5-round detachable box magazine
OPERATION: bolt action
MUZZLE VELOCITY: 2755 fps (840 mps)
EFFECTIVE RANGE: 3280 feet (1000 m) plus
CYCLIC RATE OF FIRE: not applicable

L1A1 Self-loading Rifle

The persuasive qualities of the Belgian FN FAL rifle led the British Army to adopt it as their standard service rifle from 1954, but license-produced as the L1A1 Self-loading Rifle. The L1A1 had its dimensions slightly altered to suit manufacture in imperial measurements and would only fire semi-automatic. The L1A1 served British soldiers well across the world. On the streets of Northern Ireland, it was over-powerful, as it could easily command ranges of more than 2624 feet (800 m). Yet it left its mark in the Falklands War, when it could easily handle the distances between Argentine and British positions. The L1A1 was, however, a fearsome weapon to handle and needed substantial training. Although replaced by the 5.56 mm L85A1 in the 1980s, it was used by special forces units in the Gulf War for its long range.

SPECIFICATIONS

COUNTRY OF ORIGIN: United Kingdom
CALIBER: 7.62 x 51 mm NATO
LENGTH: 41.54 inches (1055 mm)
WEIGHT: 9.50 pounds (4.31 kg)
BARREL: 535 mm, 4 grooves, rh
FEED: 20-round box magazine
OPERATION: gas
MUZZLE VELOCITY: 2800 fps (853 mps)
EFFECTIVE RANGE: 2624 feet (800 m) plus
CYCLIC RATE OF FIRE: semi-automatic only

Kalashnikov AKM

While the original AK-47 was a superb gun in most respects, there were problems in the quality of its stamped steel receiver that let down its potentially good reliability. In 1951, the switch was made to a machined receiver, but this then made the gun's production cost per unit rise considerably. The solution was found in 1959 in the AKM (the M stands for "Modernized"), the most prolific of the AK series, and the one most likely to be encountered when Kalashnikovs are present on the battlefield. It featured a higher quality stamped receiver ideal for the gun and it also took on several other minor improvements. These included an angled muzzle, which acted as a basic compensator to control muzzle climb, and a newly designed bayonet that could convert into a wire cutter. An AKM can usually be distinguished from an AK-47 by the recess above the magazine housing.

SPECIFICATIONS

COUNTRY OF ORIGIN: Soviet Union/Russia
CALIBER: 7.62 x 39 mm Soviet M1943
LENGTH: 34.65 inches (880 mm)
WEIGHT: 9.48 pounds (4.3 kg)
BARREL: 415 mm, 4 grooves, rh

FEED: 30-round detachable box magazine
OPERATION: gas
MUZZLE VELOCITY: 2350 fps (600 mps)
EFFECTIVE RANGE: 1312 feet (400 m)
CYCLIC RATE OF FIRE: 600 rpm

M16A1

Designed by Eugene Stoner, the M16 first appeared as the 7.62 mm AR-10, followed by the AR-15, which was rechambered for the 5.56 mm round. License to produce the AR-15 switched to Colt in 1959 and significant sales of the gun went out to Southeast Asia, the UK, and the US Army, when it was retitled the M16. However, in early service in Vietnam, it had a tendency to jam and had to be kept very clean (not easy in the jungle). The problem was found to be a new propellant that caused excessive fouling; modifications to both gun and propellant left an excellent assault rifle, the M16A1. The plastic and pressed steel construction made it relatively light and the high-velocity of the round more than compensated for its small caliber in combat.

SPECIFICATIONS

COUNTRY OF ORIGIN: United States
CALIBER: 5.56 x 45 mm M193
LENGTH: 38.98 inches (990 mm)
WEIGHT: 6.31 pounds (2.86 kg)
BARREL: 508 mm, 6 grooves, rh
FEED: 30-round detachable box magazine
OPERATION: gas
MUZZLE VELOCITY: 3280 fps (1000 mps)
EFFECTIVE RANGE: 1640 feet (500 m) plus
CYCLIC RATE OF FIRE: 800 rpm

Heckler & Koch G3

Although the G3 does not have the fame of the M16 or the AK47, it still stands as one of the most widely distributed modern assault rifles, used by more than 50 international armies. Based on a CETME design, its operation is a roller-delayed blowback with a heritage that can be traced back to Mauser in the mid-1940s. The rugged operation makes the G3 an exceptionally dependable rifle in combat, firing the powerful 7.62 mm NATO cartridge. Using the full-size rifle cartridge gave it great range and power, however, it also made it date quickly once the new 5.56 mm weapons appeared on the scene. The gun could be rather heavy and had a crude appearance because of an extensive use of metal stampings. The G3 has been thoroughly combat-tested in theatres ranging from Africa and the Middle East to South America.

SPECIFICATIONS

COUNTRY OF ORIGIN: Germany
CALIBER: 7.62 mm NATO
LENGTH: 40.35 inches (1025 mm)
WEIGHT: 9.70 pounds (4.4 kg)
BARREL: 450 mm, 4 grooves, rh
FEED: 20-round detachable box magazine
OPERATION: delayed blowback
MUZZLE VELOCITY: 2625 fps (800 mps)
EFFECTIVE RANGE: 1640 feet (500 m) plus
CYCLIC RATE OF FIRE: 500–600 rpm

FAMAS

The FAMAS is now the French forces' standard side arm and it is an all-round excellent weapon. Firing standard NATO and French Service 5.56 mm ammunition, its bullpup design (with the chamber behind the trigger) gives it good accuracy over 1,312 feet (400 m) due to the length of its barrel. Its light delayed-blowback operation, which uses a two-part bolt, permits a very high rate of fire — 900 rpm can empty the magazine in seconds — something which the trigger's lightness does nothing to control. The FAMAS started to enter French service in the early 1980s and it has given French troops a world-class firearm. The latest model, the F2, has dispensed with the trigger guard in favor of a full handguard — ideal for use with gloved hands — and it will also take the M16 magazine, now almost an essential feature of NATO weapons.

SPECIFICATIONS

COUNTRY OF ORIGIN: France
CALIBER: 5.56 mm NATO or Type France
LENGTH: 29.80 inches (757 mm)
WEIGHT: 7.96 pounds (3.61 kg)
BARREL: 488 mm, 3 grooves, rh
FEED: 25-round detachable box magazine
OPERATION: gas
MUZZLE VELOCITY: 3150 fps (960 mps)
EFFECTIVE RANGE: 1312 feet (400 m)
CYCLIC RATE OF FIRE: 900–1000 rpm

Beretta SC70

The SC70 was a carbine variant of the AR70, designed for greater portability and use within confined areas such as buildings and vehicles. In most respects it is not much different than the standard rifle, except that it had a folding metal butt stock that could be collapsed for ease of storage when required. With the butt folded, the overall length of the gun was taken down to 28.97 inches (736 mm). The SC70 also led to a weapon, the SC70 Short, which had the main dimensions reduced, in a similar way to the Soviet AKSU-74. The SC70 Short had a 320 mm barrel, which reduced its overall accuracy but, combined with the folding metal stock, made the gun very convenient for use on covert or security operations when a weapon had to have limited visible presence.

SPECIFICATIONS
COUNTRY OF ORIGIN: Italy
CALIBER: 5.56 x 45 mm NATO
LENGTH: 37.79 inches (960 mm) stock extended; 28.97 inches (736 mm) stock folded
WEIGHT: 8.37 pounds (3.8 kg)
BARREL: 452 mm
FEED: 30-round detachable box magazine
OPERATION: gas
MUZZLE VELOCITY: 3180 fps (962 mps)
EFFECTIVE RANGE: 2624 feet (800 m)
CYCLIC RATE OF FIRE: 630 rpm

Barrett Light Fifty M82A1

The Barrett Light Fifty M82A1 is a truly fearsome sniper weapon, firing a .50 caliber Browning Machine Gun (BMG) round over distances of up to and over a mile. The destructive force of the .50 caliber round makes it decisive in both anti-personnel and anti-materiel roles. A semi-automatic, short-recoil weapon working off an 11-round box magazine; the Barrett controls its recoil mainly through a large muzzle brake, which diverts some 30 percent of its gases out at right angles to the direction of the barrel. The highly specialist nature of the weapon has somewhat limited its use and it is almost entirely in the hands of US special forces, although some have even turned up in terrorist use in Northern Ireland. It also saw service in the Persian Gulf, where it proved a useful weapon over long ranges. It was, however, not the only .50 caliber sniper rifle on the market and production of this particular weapon ceased in 1992.

SPECIFICATIONS

COUNTRY OF ORIGIN: United States
CALIBER: .50 caliber BMG
LENGTH: 60.98 inches (1549 mm)
WEIGHT: 32.41 pounds (14.7 kg)
BARREL: 838 mm, 8 grooves, rh
FEED: 11-round box magazine
OPERATION: short-recoil, semi-automatic
MUZZLE VELOCITY: 2800 fps (843 mps)
EFFECTIVE RANGE: 3280 feet (1000 m) plus
CYCLIC RATE OF FIRE: not applicable

QBZ-95

Having lagged behind the rest of the world in terms of assault rifle design, in the 1990s, China revealed the QBZ-95 as a new generation of infantry firepower. The impetus behind the rifle was the development of a 5.8 x 42 mm cartridge during the late 1980s, which Chinese designers claimed had superior performance to its Western rival, the 5.56 x 45 mm NATO. The QBZ-95 was one of a family of weapons created to take the new cartridge. It is of bullpup layout and is a gas-operated, rotating-bolt rifle. The carrying handle at the top of the gun also incorporates an integral rear sight, although the gun can also take external optical or night-vision sights. Underbelly fitment includes a bayonet or a grenade launcher. Other members of the family include sniper, carbine, and light support (bipod-mounted) weapons.

SPECIFICATIONS

COUNTRY OF ORIGIN: China
CALIBER: 5.8 x 42 mm
LENGTH: 29.92 inches (760 mm)
WEIGHT: 749 pounds (3.4 kg)
BARREL: 520 mm
FEED: 30-round detachable box magazine
OPERATION: gas, rotating bolt
MUZZLE VELOCITY: n/a
EFFECTIVE RANGE: 1640 feet (500 m)
CYCLIC RATE OF FIRE: 650 rpm

Heckler & Koch G36

The G36 was a development intended to take over from the HK33 assault rifle. It was unveiled in 1997, and in it, Heckler & Koch have moved away from the roller-locked delayed blowback operation of their previous assault rifles to a gas-operated system of a type similar to that used in the Armalite AR-18. The G36 comes in three versions: a standard G36 rifle with bipod, the G36K carbine with more compact dimensions for vehicular and special forces use, and the MG36, which is actually a heavy-barrelled light support weapon. A number of European countries have adopted the G36 as a standard weapon, and by most accounts it is an excellent, accurate weapon.

SPECIFICATIONS
COUNTRY OF ORIGIN: Germany
CALIBER: 5.56 x 45 mm NATO
LENGTH: 39.33 inches (999 mm) stock extended; 29.84 inches (758 mm) stock folded
WEIGHT: 7.49 pounds (3.4 kg)
BARREL: 480 mm, 6 grooves, rh
FEED: 30-round detachable box magazine
OPERATION: gas
MUZZLE VELOCITY: not available
EFFECTIVE RANGE: not available
CYCLIC RATE OF FIRE: 750 rpm

M39

The M39 is a replacement for the Designated Marksman Rifle (DMR) in US Marine Corps service. Although it has a technologically advanced appearance, its ancestry in the M14 rifle is still evident. It is intended for use by Marine marksmen, soldiers specially trained to take shots out to and beyond 2624 feet (800 m). The M49 fires the 7.62 x 51 mm NATO round (although of match-grade M118LR 175- grain Long Range variety), and is a gas-operated, rotating-bolt design fed from a 20-round box magazine. Its semi-auto capability may not give the accuracy of some bolt-action designs, but it provides the reassurance of back-up firepower if an engagement moves to close quarters. Standard features of the M39 include a variable-length stock, adjustable comb (cheek-piece), a MIL-STD-1913 Picatinny rail for the mounting of scopes and other aiming devices, and a Harris folding bipod.

SPECIFICATIONS

COUNTRY OF ORIGIN: United States
CALIBER: 7.62 x 51 mm NATO
LENGTH: 44.21 inches (1123 mm)
WEIGHT: 16.53 pounds (7.5 kg)
BARREL: 559 mm
FEED: 20-round detachable box magazine
OPERATION: gas
MUZZLE VELOCITY: 2832 fps (863 mps)
EFFECTIVE RANGE: 2624 feet (800 m)
CYCLIC RATE OF FIRE: not applicable

Sterling L2A1

The Sterling's signature curved 34-round magazine, 50-year plus service record and its use by more than 90 nations have made it one of the most famous firearms of the twentieth century. It first entered service in the British Army in 1953 as the Sterling L2A1, with the L2A2 and L2A3 appearing in 1953 and 1956, respectively. The Sterling is a resilient and hard-working gun. Its recoil was kept under control by an advanced primer ignition system that actually fired the round a fraction of a second before the round seated itself in the chamber, the breech block then being carried backwards by the leftover force. The Sterling became a standard issue submachine gun across the world and is still made under license in India, although Sterling ceased trading in 1988.

SPECIFICATIONS

COUNTRY OF ORIGIN: United Kingdom
CALIBER: 9 mm Parabellum
LENGTH: 27.16 inches (690 mm) stock extended; 19.02 inches (483 mm) stock folded
WEIGHT: 5.99 pounds (2.72 kg)
BARREL: 198 mm, 6 grooves, rh
FEED: 34-round detachable box magazine
OPERATION: blowback
MUZZLE VELOCITY: 1295 fps (395 mps)
EFFECTIVE RANGE: 230 feet (70 m)
CYCLIC RATE OF FIRE: 550 rpm

Uzi

Beloved of Hollywood thrillers, few weapons have entered into the popular vocabulary or global service as much as the Uzi. It was designed by the talented Lieutenant Uziel Gal in the early years of Israel's existence, when Israel was desperate for a native-produced submachine gun. Gal based his design around the wraparound bolt system found in the Czech vz 23 series, in which the bolt is actually placed forward of the chamber on firing, thus saving a great deal of space and allowing for a longer barrel. Gal's design was an intense success. Simply made and operated, the Uzi is easily held and packs a potent rate of fire. It initially came with a wooden stock, but now a folding metal stock is standard. Used by more than 26 countries outside of Israel, the Uzi has made a definite impact on twentieth-century weapons development.

SPECIFICATIONS

COUNTRY OF ORIGIN: Israel
CALIBER: 9 mm Parabellum
LENGTH: 25.59 inches (650 mm) stock extended; 18.50 inches (470 mm) stock folded
WEIGHT: 8.15 pounds (3.7 kg)
BARREL: 260 mm, 4 grooves, rh
FEED: 25- or 32-round box magazine
OPERATION: blowback
MUZZLE VELOCITY: 1312 fps (400 mps)
EFFECTIVE RANGE: 394 feet (120 m)
CYCLIC RATE OF FIRE: 600 rpm

Beretta Model 12

A Domenico Salza design, the Model 12 emerged in the mid-1950s. Although Beretta now increased the use of metal stampings to reduce cost, overall quality of the weapon was still retained, this time applied to the tubular receiver design. The Model 12's operation was an orthodox blowback, with the use of a "wraparound" bolt to reduce the gun length. The receiver was larger than normal to accommodate the bolt that surrounded the barrel, and had two plastic pistol grips at either end, with the magazine in between. The fire selector was a push-through type, and there were two safeties: one conventional, and one below the trigger guard. Accurate and incredibly hardy, the Model 12 found most use with Italian Special Forces and also in the Middle East, Africa, and South America, with licensed production in Brazil and Saudi Arabia.

SPECIFICATIONS

COUNTRY OF ORIGIN: Italy
CALIBER: 9 mm Parabellum
LENGTH: 25.98 inches (660 mm) wooden stock; 25.39 inches (645 mm) metal stock extended; 16.37 inches (416 mm) metal stock folded
WEIGHT: 6.50 pounds (2.95 kg)
BARREL: 203 mm, 6 grooves, rh
FEED: 20-, 30- or 40-round box magazine
OPERATION: blowback
MUZZLE VELOCITY: 1247 fps (380 mps)
EFFECTIVE RANGE: 394 feet (120 m)
CYCLIC RATE OF FIRE: 550 rpm

Sterling L34A1

Development of a silenced version of the Sterling L2 began as far back as 1956, with both Patchett and the Royal Armaments Research & Development Establishment (RARDE) producing prototypes. The latter went through to acceptance and became the Sterling L34A1. The integral suppressor is very effective; the barrel has 72 radial holes drilled into it and is surrounded by a metal cylinder containing baffles into which the firing gases expand and swirl. As with all silencers, muzzle velocity is substantially reduced, but this does not compromise the L34A1 as an effective weapon. Indeed, with recoil lessened, the bolt and recoil spring were lightened, thus making the weapon much more manageable on full-auto than its non-silenced counterpart. Used mainly by special forces soldiers, the L34A1 provides a practical silenced weapon, which promises good performance.

SPECIFICATIONS

COUNTRY OF ORIGIN: United Kingdom
CALIBER: 9 mm Parabellum
LENGTH: 34.02 inches (864 mm) stock extended; 25.98 inches (660 mm) stock folded
WEIGHT: 7.94 pounds (3.6 kg)
BARREL: 198 mm, 6 grooves, rh
FEED: 34-round detachable box magazine
OPERATION: blowback
MUZZLE VELOCITY: 984 fps (300 mps)
EFFECTIVE RANGE: 120 m (120 m)
CYCLIC RATE OF FIRE: 515 rpm

M60

Despite being the dominant US Army GPMG from Vietnam to the Gulf War, the M60's history is full of problems. Developed in the late 1950s, it was an amalgam of Germany's MG42 and FG42 respectively. Despite this, and features such as the Stellite linings on the barrels that allow firing even when the barrel is white hot, the M60 was plagued by deficiencies. Barrel change was awkward as there was no handle and each barrel had its own cylinder and bipod. Thus the firer had to wrestle with the red-hot barrel using an asbestos glove (easily lost during combat). The M60E1 had its own barrel handle and kept the bipod and gas-cylinder separate, however, gas-operation was prone to fouling and jamming (leading soldiers in Vietnam to call it "the Pig"). Despite its inefficiencies, the M60 stayed in widespread service for several decades before being phased out.

SPECIFICATIONS
COUNTRY OF ORIGIN: United States
CALIBER: 7.62 mm NATO
LENGTH: 43.75 inches (1110 mm)
WEIGHT: 22.93 pounds (10.4 kg)
BARREL: 560 mm, 4 grooves, rh

FEED: disintegrating-link belt
OPERATION: gas, air-cooled
MUZZLE VELOCITY: 2805 fps (855 mps)
EFFECTIVE RANGE: 9843 feet (3000 m) plus
CYCLIC RATE OF FIRE: 600 rpm

L7A2

Made by Belgian arms producer Fabrique Nationale, the FN MAG was first designed in the 1950s by M. Ernest Vervier and has been used or made under license in more than 80 countries. The weapon's name is an abbreviation for Mitrailleuse d'Appui Général, meaning general purpose machine gun (GPMG). In the United Kingdom, it was made under license as the L7A1 and later the L7A2; more than 80 other countries have also taken it into their forces. The L7 was adopted by the British Army as a replacement for the long-serving Vickers machine gun and the Bren, following trials in 1957. The FN MAG can be mounted on both its own front bipod for the light support roles or a heavy tripod for sustained fire deployments. It was this reliability that influenced the US Army into deciding to develop the MAG as their M240 series GPMG, replacing the M60 machine gun.

SPECIFICATIONS

COUNTRY OF ORIGIN: Belgium
CALIBER: 7.62 mm x 51 mm NATO
LENGTH: 49.72 inches (1263 mm)
WEIGHT: 23.92 pounds (10.85 kg)
BARREL: 543 mm
FEED: metal-link belt, various lengths
OPERATION: gas, air-cooled
MUZZLE VELOCITY: 2800 fps (853 mps)
EFFECTIVE RANGE: 2624 feet (800 m)
CYCLIC RATE OF FIRE: 650–1000 rpm

7.62mm Maschinengewehr 3

The 7.62 mm Maschinengewehr 3 (MG3) is instantly recognizable as a derivative of the revered MG42. During the 1950s, the German Army assessed international weaponry for its rearmament and found that the MG42 was yet to be surpassed. Thus the MG1 was produced, almost identical in every way to the MG42, with fractional changes to feed mechanism and bolt. An evolving chain of upgrades and modifications ensued (in particular, the shift to the 7.62 mm NATO rounds), leading to the current MG3, the standard light machine gun used by the German forces and many other armies around the world. The MG3 retains the original MG42's high rate of fire, although this can be varied with the use of the V550 bolt or the heavier V950 bolt. The feed can equally accept German DM1 and DM13 belts and US M13 belts.

SPECIFICATIONS

COUNTRY OF ORIGIN: Germany
CALIBER: 7.62 x 51 mm NATO
LENGTH: 48.03 inches (1220 mm)
WEIGHT: 25.35 pounds (11.5 kg)
BARREL: 531 mm, 4 grooves, rh
FEED: belt feed
OPERATION: short recoil, air-cooled
MUZZLE VELOCITY: 2690 fps (820 mps)
EFFECTIVE RANGE: 9843 feet (3000 m) plus
CYCLIC RATE OF FIRE: 1300 rpm (V550 bolt); 950 rpm (V950 bolt)

PKM 7.62mm

The PK established the general-purpose machine gun within the ranks of the Soviet Army and its variations equip Russian and many other armies around the world to this day. The gun is simplicity itself, being based on the Kalashnikov rotary-bolt system and having very few internal parts. Those parts work well, however, whether used in light-support or sustained-fire roles. The PK's one oddity is its use of the old M91 (1891) rimmed cartridge, which can generate some feed problems, but does outreach the M1943 round. The PK series is extensive, but each version is mainly distinguished by mountings. The PKM is rather different, in that the weight of the barrel is reduced and there is a greater use of stampings. It and later models can be visually separated from the others by their unfluted barrel.

SPECIFICATIONS

COUNTRY OF ORIGIN: Soviet Union/Russia
CALIBER: 7.62 x 39 mm M1943
LENGTH: 45.67 inches (1160 mm)
WEIGHT: 19.84 pounds (9 kg)
BARREL: 658 mm, 4 grooves, rh
FEED: 100-, 200- or 250-round belt
OPERATION: gas, air-cooled
MUZZLE VELOCITY: 2600 fps (800 mps)
EFFECTIVE RANGE: 6562 feet (2000 m) plus
CYCLIC RATE OF FIRE: 710 rpm

Minigun M134

The M134 Minigun sits at the far edge of the category "small arms", as it was only intended for mounted use in helicopters. Its rotating six-barrelled configuration harks back to Gatling's famous machine gun, but in this case power is supplied by an electric motor. The result is a rate of fire that can reach up to 6000 rpm. This awesome firepower was brought into action specifically for the Vietnam War. Here the Minigun was clamped either into helicopter door positions or in special gun pods, and they were used for spraying the jungle floor with 7.62 mm slugs. Each barrel has its own bolt unit and the feed is from a 4000-round belt which is usually stored in a drum. For sheer fire-to-size ratio, the Mingun takes some beating. It has made a number of appearances in Hollywood films.

SPECIFICATIONS

COUNTRY OF ORIGIN: United States
CALIBER: 7.62 x 51 mm NATO
LENGTH: 31.49 inches (800 mm)
WEIGHT: 35.05 pounds (15.9 kg)
BARREL: 559 mm, 4 grooves, rh
FEED: 4000-round link belt feed
OPERATION: electrically powered revolver
MUZZLE VELOCITY: 2850 fps (869 mps)
EFFECTIVE RANGE: 9843 feet (3000 m) plus
CYCLIC RATE OF FIRE: up to 6000 rpm

AGS-17

The AGS-17 is one of a series of belt-fed automatic grenade launchers that emerged in various world armies from the 1960s onwards. Unlike the similar US 40 mm Mark 19, which it resembled, the AGS-17 came in 30 mm, although it did also operate on the basis of a blowback action. The recoil forces of this operation were controlled through the mount, and the AGS-17 could be either used as an infantry weapon or operated from a helicopter or vehicle platform. The feed system used on the gun was belt feed, and this enabled the operator to lay down a systematic bombardment on targets to ranges of up to 3937 feet (1200 m). In this capacity, it was used to lethal effect against the guerrilla fighters in Afghanistan's mountainous terrain during the Soviet occupation of the country in the 1980s.

SPECIFICATIONS

COUNTRY OF ORIGIN: Soviet Union/Russia
CALIBER: 30 mm
LENGTH: 33.07 inches (840 mm)
WEIGHT: 39.68 pounds (18 kg) without tripod
BARREL: not available
FEED: belt feed
OPERATION: blowback, automatic
MUZZLE VELOCITY: not known
EFFECTIVE RANGE: 3937 feet (1200 m)
CYCLIC RATE OF FIRE: not known

Mk 19 Grenade Launcher

The Mk 19 Grenade Launcher became a popular harassing tool against the Vietcong during the Vietnam War. There it was first mounted onto a number of US river patrol craft used to control the Vietnamese coastline, which could bombard enemy positions ranged along the river bank with a stream of high-explosive 40 mm grenades. This proved to be an effective application for the weapon and the Mark 19's customers increased to include the US Army and Israeli forces, with both finding the Mark 19 a useful and deadly weapon when placed on vehicle mountings. A blowback grenade launcher capable of full-automatic fire feeding from a disintegrating link belt-feed, it fires from an open bolt (the bolt stays back from the chamber between firing), which helps the weapon to stay cool when firing repeatedly without pause.

SPECIFICATIONS

COUNTRY OF ORIGIN: United States
CALIBER: 40 mm
LENGTH: 40.47 inches (1028 mm)
WEIGHT: 74.96 pounds (34 kg)
BARREL: not available
FEED: belt feed, disintegrating-link belt
OPERATION: blowback
MUZZLE VELOCITY: 790 fps (240 mps)
EFFECTIVE RANGE: 5249 feet (1600 m)
CYCLIC RATE OF FIRE: not applicable

Brunswick RAW

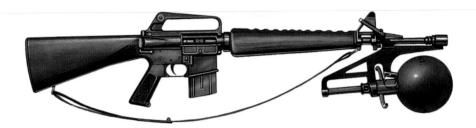

The Brunswick Rifleman's Assault Weapon (RAW) has been nicknamed the "softball from hell". The unusual spherical bomb is fired from the M16 rifle and is intended for use against light vehicles and in urban settings. In flight, the bomb is rocket assisted; when it strikes the target, its contents — 2.79 pounds (1.27 kg) of high explosives — are plastered onto the surface, then detonated (rather like the HESH shell used by tanks). The results are admittedly impressive, as it can blow its way through nearly 8 inches (200 mm) of reinforced concrete. The capabilities of the RAW are somewhat lessened by the awkwardness of its shape and attachment. It is undoubtedly useful for short-range urban combat roles and its explosive power is greater than the M203.

SPECIFICATIONS
COUNTRY OF ORIGIN: United States
CALIBER: 140 mm
LENGTH: 12 inches (305 mm)
WEIGHT: 8.36 pounds (3.8 kg)
BARREL: not applicable
FEED: single round
OPERATION: rifle fired
MUZZLE VELOCITY: 590 fps (180 mps)
EFFECTIVE RANGE: 656 feet (200 m) plus
CYCLIC RATE OF FIRE: not applicable

Remington M870

Remington has had a long history of manufacturing firearms in all weapon types, not least of which are shotguns. Its M870 series of guns has been extensively used for police and military work across the world, particularly for riot and close-quarter operations. Perhaps the defining military model was the M870 Mk 1. This was adopted by the US Marines Corps in the mid-1960s. It was a standard pump-action shotgun that was durable, powerful, had a good magazine capacity (seven rounds) and was decisive in putting a man down at close range. This killing force was tested in anger in Vietnam by Marine and US Navy SEAL teams. It could fire standard shot, flechettes, solid slugs or various other forms of ammunition. The Mk 1 still serves today around the world in assorted roles, alongside a broad family of other M870 weapons.

SPECIFICATIONS

COUNTRY OF ORIGIN: United States
CALIBER: 12 gauge
LENGTH: 41.73 inches (1060 mm)
WEIGHT: 7.94 pounds (3.6 kg)
BARREL: 533 mm
FEED: 7-round integral tubular magazine
OPERATION: pump action
MUZZLE VELOCITY: variable, depending on type of ammunition
EFFECTIVE RANGE: 328 feet (100 m)
CYCLIC RATE OF FIRE: not applicable

Pancor Jackhammer

The space-age appearance of the Pancor Jackhammer denotes its place amongst a new breed of combat shotguns. It is set in a bullpup configuration with the 10-round "ammunition cassette" set behind the trigger group. This cassette is a revolver-feed magazine, which, once emptied, is detached and replaced by a new cassette ready to fire. The old cassette is not reloaded, neither is there any ejection of rounds, they are simply retained inside the cassette. Each cassette comes pre-loaded in sealed packaging, which denotes the type of ammunition within. The Jackhammer has a gas-operated system, which, on full-automatic setting, is capable of a cyclic rate of fire of 240 rpm. Unlike many other automatic shotguns, the Jackhammer can sustain this fire owing to an effective muzzle compensator and a very rugged construction in steel and high-impact plastics.

SPECIFICATIONS

COUNTRY OF ORIGIN: United States
CALIBER: 12 gauge
LENGTH: 30 inches (762 mm)
WEIGHT: 10.08 pounds (4.57 kg) loaded
BARREL: 457 mm
FEED: 10-round detachable pre-loaded rotary cassette
OPERATION: gas
MUZZLE VELOCITY: variable, depending on type of a mmunition
EFFECTIVE RANGE: 656 feet (200 m) plus
CYCLIC RATE OF FIRE: 240 rpm

Benelli M4 Super 90

The Italian Benelli M4 was the winner of a 1990s competition to provide a new combat shotgun for the US armed forces, and from 1999 on it became a service shotgun in the US Marine Corps. Working on a semi-auto, gas-operated system (it has dual self-cleaning gas pistons for increased reliability), the M4 resembles a traditional shotgun only in its 12-gauge caliber. As well as a variety of camouflage finishes, the gun comes with a drilled and tapped receiver with Picatinny rail as standard. Its basic sight is an M4 Tactical rear ghost ring sight, adjustable for windage and elevation, and a front post, but the rail means the shotgun can take many other optical sights. Magazine capacity of the tubular, under-barrel magazine is eight rounds, plus an additional round in the chamber if so chosen. The stock is collapsible.

SPECIFICATIONS

COUNTRY OF ORIGIN: Italy
CALIBER: 120-gauge
LENGTH: 39.76 inches (1010 mm) stock extended
WEIGHT: 8.37 pounds (3.8 kg)
BARREL: 470 mm
FEED: 8-round tubular magazine
OPERATION: gas
MUZZLE VELOCITY: varies according to cartridge type
EFFECTIVE RANGE: varies according to cartridge type
CYCLIC RATE OF FIRE: not applicable

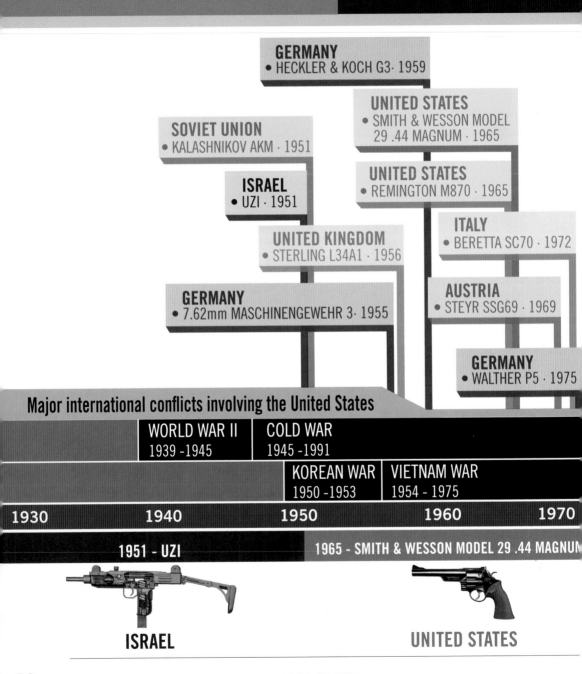

GERMANY
- HECKLER & KOCH G3 · 1959

UNITED STATES
- SMITH & WESSON MODEL 29 .44 MAGNUM · 1965

SOVIET UNION
- KALASHNIKOV AKM · 1951

UNITED STATES
- REMINGTON M870 · 1965

ISRAEL
- UZI · 1951

UNITED KINGDOM
- STERLING L34A1 · 1956

ITALY
- BERETTA SC70 · 1972

AUSTRIA
- STEYR SSG69 · 1969

GERMANY
- 7.62mm MASCHINENGEWEHR 3· 1955

GERMANY
- WALTHER P5 · 1975

Major international conflicts involving the United States

| WORLD WAR II 1939 -1945 | COLD WAR 1945 -1991 | | |
| KOREAN WAR 1950 -1953 | VIETNAM WAR 1954 - 1975 | |

| 1930 | 1940 | 1950 | 1960 | 1970 |

1951 - UZI

1965 - SMITH & WESSON MODEL 29 .44 MAGNUM

ISRAEL

UNITED STATES

FEATURED WEAPONS TIMELINE

This timeline features notable advancements in military technologies by influential nations worldwide.

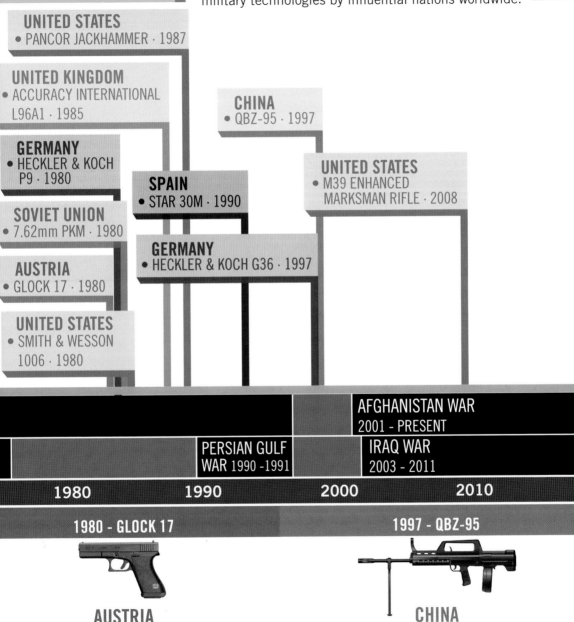

UNITED STATES
- PANCOR JACKHAMMER · 1987

UNITED KINGDOM
- ACCURACY INTERNATIONAL L96A1 · 1985

CHINA
- QBZ-95 · 1997

GERMANY
- HECKLER & KOCH P9 · 1980

SPAIN
- STAR 30M · 1990

UNITED STATES
- M39 ENHANCED MARKSMAN RIFLE · 2008

SOVIET UNION
- 7.62mm PKM · 1980

GERMANY
- HECKLER & KOCH G36 · 1997

AUSTRIA
- GLOCK 17 · 1980

UNITED STATES
- SMITH & WESSON 1006 · 1980

AFGHANISTAN WAR
2001 - PRESENT

PERSIAN GULF WAR 1990 -1991

IRAQ WAR
2003 - 2011

1980   1990   2000   2010

1980 - GLOCK 17

1997 - QBZ-95

AUSTRIA

CHINA

Glossary

assault rifle
military firearm that can switch between semiautomatic and fully automatic fire

ballistics
the science of the propulsion, flight, and impact of projectiles

barrel
the long, metal tube that the bullet is propelled through when it is fired

compaction
the process of making something smaller

counter ambush
measures taken to prevent the attack or devise surprise attack measures

electromagnetic
a magnetic field created with electricity instead of iron

electromagnetic acceleration
energy produced due to the moving rate of an electric charge

long-range round
ammunition made to be fired for a distant target

magazine
a device for holding ammunition

militia
citizen soldiers as opposed to professional soldiers

NATO (North Atlantic Treaty Organization)
a military alliance of European and North American democratic nations founded after World War II. It was designed to strengthen international ties (especially between the United States and European countries), and to serve as a counter-balance to the Soviet Union and its allied countries.

percussion
a sharp blow that detonates an artillery shell

propellants
explosives used to propel a projectile from a gun

semi-automatic rifle
A rifle that fires a cartridge each time the trigger is pulled

submachine gun
a lightweight automatic gun that shoots pistol ammunition

suppressive fire
firing at an enemy force to make them unable to fulfill their mission

telescoping bolt
one section of the bolt slides inside a larger section, which reduces the length of a weapon

telescopic sight
device used on a firearm to give an accurate point of aim

urban combat
warfare conducted in towns and cities

Vietnam War (1954-1975)
a military conflict between the Communist forces of North Vietnam supported by China and the Soviet Union and the non-Communist forces of South Vietnam supported by the United States

Further Information

Websites

http://usmilitary.about.com/od/armyweapons/l/aainfantry1.htmbasic
View photos with descriptions of small arms used by the U.S. Army.

http://www.globalsecurity.org/military/systems/ground/small-arms.htm
This site explains what small arms are and defines their use in warfare.

http://www.defensemedianetwork.com/stories/usmc-small-arms-developments/
Current small arms and the development of new small arms for the US Marine Corps.

http://www.military.com/army-birthday/history-of-us-army-weapons.html
Provides a comprehensive history of the use of small arms in US Army history.

Books

Hogg, Ian and John Weeks. *Military Small Arms of the 20th Century.* Arms and Armour Press, 1973.
A complete reference guide to small arms used by military units during this era.

Laemlein, Tom and Dale Dye. *US Small Arms in World War II.* Osprey Publishing, Limited, 2011.
A photographic history of the weapons in action during World War II.

Miller, David. *Ultimate Handguns.* Sterling, 2009.
A visual encyclopedia of over 500 handguns, from the 18th to the 21st century.

Walter, John. *Modern Machine Guns.* Greenhill Books, 2006.
A survey of machine guns in the modern era.

Index of Small Arms Profile Pages